T0196037

Nathaniel Cole Noland

WESTBOW
PRESS®
A DIVISION OF THOMAS NELSON
& ZONDERVAN

WestBow Press books may be ordered through booksellers or by contacting:

WestBow Press
A Division of Thomas Nelson & Zondervan
1663 Liberty Drive
Bloomington, IN 47403
www.westbowpress.com
844-714-3454

Scripture quotations marked KJV are taken from the King James Version.

ISBN: 978-1-6642-0123-1 (sc)
ISBN: 978-1-6642-0124-8 (hc)
ISBN: 978-1-6642-0122-4 (e)

Library of Congress Control Number: 2020914602

Print information available on the last page.

WestBow Press rev. date: 9/17/2020

Contents

Silence

3/18/1996

It's not often that beauty will hold a poet's tongue,
Thus ceasing the words that would otherwise flow.
It appears that although I have engraved images of you
warming my thoughts,
I am left with inadequate verse and rendered helpless
while trying to articulate the beauty that I behold!
And if words left unsaid are a compliment,
then I've already said far too much.
Now I favor my fear of describing you
because I'm sure that all of my attempts will fail.
If I can't express myself with pure eloquence,
I'll fall far short of my intent,
and those efforts would be unworthy
of such a beautiful, deserving soul.
Since it's beyond my control, I've let it go.
I can only give you what my weakened lips can offer.
All I can adduce, right here, right now,
Is encased in this:
my underscored praise
in silence …

***

This details my failure to write about the beauty of my friend, Caroline. All I could remember about my first encounter with her was that she had beautiful eyes and an incredibly beautiful soul.

She was so beautiful inside that I couldn't remember the color of her eyes or what she was wearing. I felt a little embarrassed that I couldn't remember her features. I admit that I was proud of myself also for only caring about what she looked like on the inside.

This was a simple attempt on my part to capture that overpowering beauty that she possesses. Though I tried to write, I kept falling short of a worthy description of her inner beauty. In the poem, I finally relent and say that all I can do is praise her with my overwhelming silence.

In case you are wondering, she is incredibly beautiful on the outside too.

Caroline, I love you!

Don't change
to live in this world.
Live to change it!

Don't look for someone
you'd be willing to die for.
Look for someone
you'd be willing to live for.

I've come to the realization
that I've only a very vague idea
about what is really going on.

Love, patience, understanding—is there anything else you really need?

I'm unworthy of all the trials you've put me through and the lessons I've learned from them.

I'm not smarter or better than you.
I'm just at a different level of understanding.
That doesn't necessarily mean that I'm any higher.

Man can only achieve his greatest feats
when he allows his spirit's greatest strengths
to overcome his mind's greatest weaknesses.

I gave both of my sons suitcases, but I never wanted to see either one of them go.

I'm only the man that I imagine I am.

I'm more like me than I know.

I can never love anyone as much as I truly want to.

Voices

9/14/2018

Hanging branches
moving along with the flowing breeze.
Leaves whispering to those who pass.
"My love is one of ease."
So I whisper back,
"I just love hearing the voices of trees."

The ocean lies beside me,
manifesting this beach.
I pace myself, just enough so
that I can hear one voice saying,
"Walk in peace.
Look beyond the chaos created by man."
I whisper back,
"I'm beginning to understand."

Another voice says,
"I am here asking you if you can hear me now.
I'm uttering to your soul.
I'm not concerned with all of your choices.
I am all you need to know.
Am I being just a little too subtle?"

A butterfly's wings
always sing,
"Optimality can erupt in silence."

"Just listen for my spoken words.
They are everywhere.
Don't fail to hear these oratorical susurrations.
They aren't just my many attempts
to gently reach you.
They are but just a few examples
of my many voices."

Ten

7/16/2018

Ten fingers
for ten laws.
One for each
to remember them all.
Ten tools to use
to break any of them and fall.
Ten toes
to keep your balance
so you can run away
so you won't sin.
One lifetime
to save one soul.
Ten fingers
to help you pray
so He'll let you in.
One savior to guide you.
He is the circle,
the keeper
of ten.

Reflection

5/6/1999

You have said that I am beautiful.
I agree with you because it's very true.
But it's only because I've been captured
by your essence.
Now I'm only a reflection of you.
I'm the mirror standing here before you.
Your reflection is all that you see.
It was far too much beauty for this mirror to hold,
so I reflect you and set beauty free!

Renowned

1/28/2019

At night, the night does not grieve.
The moon is still aglow.
Perpetually coming around,
Sunsets should not fade from memory;
The photo ops are in their place.
Moments rise to be renowned to bring glory to their king.
They are jewels upon His crown.
The lights, these lights know not, are going down.
They are not slaves bound to the descriptions of this world.
Looking from the universal point of view,
There is no up or down.
Up is at God's discretion.

Mother Nature will keep you on your toes,
and if you don't watch out,
Father Time will knock you off your feet.

The heart is the strongest muscle because it's the only place that can hold love.

We don't need to see someone to forgive them.
We don't need to see him to be forgiven either.

At night, we still have many lights to guide us.

We all serve our roles,
even if we never realize it.

We're always surrounded by love.
We just have to be open enough to feel it.

My mom is the best woman I've ever known.
It's not always easy to understand her,
but she's hardly ever been proven wrong.

My greatest quality is humility.
My greatest strength is love.
Love always humbles me.

If you've ever had your heart broken,
don't try to protect it by closing it up.
Your heart did what it was created to do:
it kept loving.

The Weeping Willow

8/20/2018

The willow cries …

Do you see the small tears appearing as leaves,
growing on its hanging branches?

The willow embodies many chances.
That's why it cries for each of those lives
who admire its modesty.

It's for those who are innocent
and those who are cautious in their presence.

The willow weeps
with no sense of judgment.

So open yourself—
there's always more to marvel at,
even in your shortest travels.

The leaves spring out and flow down
like a city's featured fountain.

If you see this tree weeping for you,
cry along with it.
For that call belongs
to the weeping willow.

***

Care enough about everyone that you are willing to cry with them and for them in their time of need.

Faster Than Light

8/23/2017

Some people find lightning
quite frightening.
On the other hand,
some are very fond of that light.

It's a glorious manifestation,
an occurrence in life
that can only be found in the sky.

Light strikes
at the tapestry
blanketing a marvelous sky!

The lights, the veins of the storm,
pulse, feeding it
with supernatural life.

We all need
this magnificent lesson
of the power that comes from light.

There's the rumbling
that comes after the boom
as the thunder comes crashing in.

Every time
the lightning strikes,
I hope it will never end.

Each mighty event
is an awakening,
using nature to remind us
what is always right.

There is no real mystery
in this world that is mightier or faster.
Nothing is greater than light!

Consuming Silence

3/24/2020

This is my first draft of *Consuming Silence*. I call this a poem's seed. 3/24/20

Must you interrupt me while I'm in the midst of consuming silence?
You're starting to make it taste a bit bitter.
Can't you see this meal is a key, a necessity, for my survival?
I find it's flavor to be oh so sweet!
In tasting, I've discovered that silence lacks not its own tone.
Let's wonder. Why can't you seem to hear it?
It's a beautiful melody that notes bemoan a travesty,
Once the delicate seal between heart and soul has been thoughtlessly
Transgressed, and so ruefully broken.
So listen carefully to the song it plays, for once heard,
Your soul will refuse to let it be forgotten.
Ssh. Open your heart and soul for now, all you need do, is listen.

I wanted my readers to see how a small idea can grow into something bigger and better. This is the final version of the poem after 5 months of looking at it, and hundreds of changes.

I call it the fruit of the poem.

Consuming Silence

Must you interrupt me,
While I'm in the midst
Of consuming silence?
Can't you see this meal
Is a necessity?
It's the key to my survival!

Here! Taste it!
You'll discover
It has its own zest.
It's own savory tone…
I find it's flavor
To be oh so sweet,
But you're starting to make it
Taste a bit bitter.

Instead of asking you
To leave me alone,
I'm inviting you
Into this moment right now,
So we can wonder together,
As to why,
You can't seem to relish in it.

You see, silence
Is a beautiful melody
With greater depth
Than the galaxies
Until it starts bemoaning
The travesty,
When an interruption breaks
The delicate seal,
Known as the union,
Of heart and soul.

Be careful…
Words confiscate inner peace.
So don't make the basic mistake
Of thinking they need to be spoken
Because the union can be
Easily transgressed
From you choosing
To use your words,
Or at the very least,
It will become ruefully broken.

So, fetter your mouth,
And embrace the moment,
Like a knife,
This will open the universe ethereally.
Dining on this eternal meal
Will orchestrate
The ballads ability
To appease a starving soul.

This regal meal is ripened
With spiritual sustenance
Which allows you to heal,
To love, and grow.
But you can't eat this dish

16

Like it's a chore.
Your spirit is obligated
To the Divine as such,
That you must
swallow it whole.

You accept these sacred gifts
Through modesty.
So, stay focused.
This is about far more
Than just listening.

You must humble yourself first
To hear the music
That abounds in silence.
It is only then,
When you can become aware
Of the spiritual diet
You are missing.

Listen, to the song
Playing right now,
Before it's reinterupted.
For once heard,
Your heart will feast,
And your soul
Will be uplifted.

This feast
Is a point of need,
And you need to feed on it
Quite often.
I promise
If you do,
The music will become
Increasingly clear,

And the quintessential sound
Will never be forgotten.
Ssh......
Hear it?

Find It

Let those who need religion find it.
Let those who seek spirituality find it.
Let those who seek neither find that as well.
I have been blessed by both.

The need for each is separate from the other and is to be respected.
Find what you need to walk in this existence.
When you find it, all is well.
We should beg one another, Peace be with you.

Forgiveness isn't for the perpetrator.
It's a necessity for the victim to truly survive.

Once you've been in the light
then step into darkness,
you cannot see at first.
Maybe that's something telling you that
you were created to be in the light.

Stop!
Calm yourself.
If you feel your heartbeat in your chest,
you're still alive.
So live!

Don't let yourself pass someone
without realizing you're not alone.
One day, they might even become your friend.

Life is an endless cycle of lessons.
If you can't learn from your current one, don't worry.
More are yet to come, and the one that you didn't learn from will eventually
come back around.

A friend is not someone you just get along with.
They are ones who'll never be out of your life.
There is someone who'll always be by your side,
and someone who'll have you in his or her thoughts.
Distance does not matter.

Parenthood is not just learning how to parent
from your parents;
it's learning how to parent from your children.

God is.
So are you.
So be.

Evanescence

8/6/1996

I never see the pain
inside my heart
until I decide to let it go.
Upon its release, it races.
It goes streaking down my face
until the pain is erased,
and I no longer feel its mark.
It splashes and dissipates

after hitting the ground,
creating an unmistakable sound.
The musical crystals
leaving my face
are playing the notes of my pain
as it's being erased.
And it's then,
in their evanescence,
that I can smile!

All tears should be welcomed. Tears of pain are mercy because they give release. With release and recognition comes the ability to move on. After you cry, you will always feel a little better.

You will never be able to release pain until you decide to face it and feel it. Once you do, you are well on your way to happiness. Simply let each drop do its job by washing away the pain inside your heart. Tears are clear notes of joy yet to be experienced. They are to be played whenever needed. Never be ashamed to cry.

The Meal

1/28/2019

Split the night from day.
Realize there is little difference.
Life is on the cutting blocks.
Sleeping or awake,
knives still cut in each of those moments.

Mix flesh with the spice of life.
You are then made ready.
You shall have your supper.

You must digest your food
before you are worthy of dessert.
When will you start to prepare your meal?
And to whom will you be serving?

***

This is about being prepared for eternity.
Realize there is not much to life or death.
They both come whether we want it or not.
They are part of the sum, split by the knife.
Our lives are always moving forward,
whether asleep or awake, dead or alive.
Life still matters at both times of a full day,
whether being active or dormant.

Mix your body, your soul, with love; then you are ready to live.
You must take in all your life experiences
before you are ready for eternity.
When will you start to live?
And are you just serving yourself or other people?

Strength in Arms

6/23/2018

A child in fear
Will seek the comfort
Of your warm embrace.
A kind, reassuring hug
Is all that it takes.
The firmness of your giving
Causes the anxiety to let go.
Realize the only power you've shown here is
The mighty strength of your love

We should never underestimate the power of a hug!

Survival/Uncovered

9/8/2018

I consume all
to quench my thirst
for knowledge.
Being caught up in it all
stalls nothing else that follows.
My thoughts rise
to meet this challenge.
My mind sighs
each time it swallows.
Each drop is a pearl
that my intellect treasures.
I polish them off to meet this hunger.
To know is survival;
it's a test I've discovered.
Is this my own shell
that my mind's eye has uncovered?

Fishing

9/10/2018

Fishing,
saying words, casting lines,
luring phrases to hit their marks.

True and current,
it is a fact;
I'm not really that smart.
On some occasions, though, I know what I'm doing.

This bait doesn't lie.
I'm not content, I refuse to die,
because I have yet to have all this food.

The Living Word kills
what it feels
is any manner of spiritual starvation.

So why haven't I eaten my catch
that is here on my plate?

It is simple.
Let me paraphrase.
I'm not done doing His work just yet,
so He told me, "Keep on fishing."

When someone hurts you,
you feel you have a reason to be vindictive.
Don't act upon it,
or you'll no longer be the victim.

Hesitation:
the mind's signal
that something is very wrong.
Sometimes it is a reassurance
that something's very good.

Love:
the higher power!

Follow the path of Christ;
He already knows the way.

Only raise your hand
To shake another.

Searching with your soul
Is the best way to see.

You're always doing one of two things in life.
You're either learning something from someone,
or
you're teaching someone something.
So learn well and always teach good lessons.

Pain
is always your ally.
It always warns you when something's wrong.
It tells you its point of entry,
and through it
is your only way out.

My Sweet Memory

3/14/1997

My pendulum,
You are balanced,
Swinging between my conscience
And my heart.
I am aware of your physical absence,
So I live in this paradox.
Although I cannot see you,
My mind still pictures you
As being very near,

And you will never fade completely
Because your voice is always there
For me to hear.
It might only be a whisper,
But that can still meet my needs,
Because I can always hear you
Or see you
As long as my heart shall beat.
With each pulse, I feed my thoughts
To build you a most delicate clasp.
It is deep, deep inside me,
Where I have created a castle
Just for you
That has crystal walls
That are as clear as any glass.
It's there that I can always see you
As a recollection of my past.
For it is a miracle
Of a sweet memory,
Until my heart,
Shall beat
Its last.

This is my attempt tell all of my friends and family members who have passed
or who are separated from me by distance that I will always hear them and see
them in my mind, and that I carry them in my heart and soul. Rest In Peace Mom,
Miguel and Grandpa Joe

Let That Sink In

1/31/2019

Question the questions.
Let that sink in.
Are all the answers in the answers?
Let that sink in.
What lies in between, in between all this?
Let that sink in.
What is the difference in these differences?
Let that sink in.
What are your opinions on my opinions?
Let that sink in.
Did I raise even one eyebrow?
I think I'll think about that, and let that sink in.

Ebb and Flow

6/24/2018

Even though I was full of this world, I had nothing to offer. My life wasn't all carved out; I was empty and lacking substance.

So I started off very weak as a little creek, yearning to be saved. Just a trickle when I came out of Your mouth, unknowing that all waterways don't find their way back home.

While learning how water works, I had to have storms come my way just so I could grow. I rose from my bed just to be taught how to ebb and flow.

You were taking me to a place I did not understand, so I was held up so my reservoir could begin to grow.

You helped this poor river by pouring me out, plotting my course, leading me to Your home.

I struggled because You kept bending me to Your will, helping me so I wouldn't flow out of control.

I relied on You, and You banked on me. You were no longer an unknown.

You released my deluge by telling me I'm deep enough to lead others on. So I gushed as You sent us out toward Your heavenly abode.

You told me how to feed from my forks, even though I'm unworthy of such a noble cause.

We are anomalies on our way, excitedly rushing in. Rising up from our beds to bend and kneel at your feet. You are so righteous that we humbly flow, approaching Your mercy seat.

We are so happy to see You there, as You sit upon Your glorious throne. Praised be, we've all just learned that we've never been alone.

We all crested and gave our best, streaming into Your sea of love. Now we're aware of how all rivers should be as we all ebb and flow.

The Eyes of My Child

5/27/2018

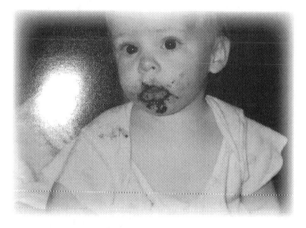

When you look
into the eyes of my child,
what do you see?

Do you see the wonderment
and innocence
that I can see
when I look
into the eyes of my child?

When you look
into the eyes of my child,
what do you see?

Do you see
what love can bring,
just like I see
when I look
into the eyes of my child?

When you look
into the eyes of my child,
what don't you see?

You don't see pain,
chaos,
or suffering
when you look
into the eyes of my child.

When you look
into the eyes of my child,
what don't you see?

You don't see any scars
or broken hearts
from lost dreams.
You see none of this

when you look
into the eyes of my child.

When you look
into the eyes of my child,
what don't you see?

You don't see the remains
of unbroken chains,
neglect,
or misery
when you look
into the eyes of my child.

When you look
into the eyes of my child,
what don't you see?

You don't see a history
of violence or abuse,
or unspoken excuses,
because you'll see they are free
when you look
into the eyes of my child.

When you look
into the eyes of my child,
what don't you see?

You don't see
negativity
or hurtful things
in their hearts,
because it's not there
when you look
into the eyes of my child.

When we look into
the eyes of my child,
what do we see?

We only see love,
joy, and freedom
in a child full of hopeful dreams.
It's easy to see
when we look
into the eyes of my child.

When we look
into the eyes of my child,
what do we see?

We see that I loved them so much,
that I kept them free,
free from all of the sins
that were passed onto me.

Why?
It's a miracle from God.
He injected them with the love
that He gave to me
so everyone can see
it is just like it's supposed to be,
when anyone looks
into the eyes
of my child!

Jared and Derek, I love you so much that I made sure that you never had to suffer
the way I suffered as a child. I'm so thankful that I had God's mercy to keep me
free from passing on evil deeds to you.

The Hunt

1/29/2019

I stalked so slowly while hunting along the creek that the red fox was almost walking under my foot before he knew something was wrong. He never saw me until he walked into my boot. He jumped, took a few quick steps, and looked back in surprise. I was just as shocked as he.

Even though I was within inches of the quails, they did not notice me. I was praying, moving slower than a mantis.

I caught the coyote trying to see me standing among the saplings, but he had no chance. I was in camouflage.
I could see him twitching his head back and forth as he tried his eyes. Then he caught my scent, so he simply walked off into the trees.

I hissed at the bobcat to let him know I was there.
He was beautiful, but I wanted him to keep his distance.

I was on the ground excited and a little scared when I saw the wolf pack coming toward me. Thankfully, they veered off in a new direction.

The great horned owl had just barely caught my eye in the snow. His wings and the moment were silent. I watched him watching me for a full ten minutes. Finally we both agreed that we were both to be respected.
The best times I've ever had while hunting are the times when I killed nothing.

Love is truth,
But that is the very thing
that can leave you feeling battered and bruised.

God has blessed me.
He gives me lessons where
it's everything I can do to handle it,
but He never gives me more than I can take.

Every moment, you can make or break
someone you come across.
So be wise with your words and actions.

Anger
originates as pain in your heart.
Then it progresses
when you can't express that hurt with your mind.

If it's dark outside to you,
it's not because the sun went down.

Don't be confused.
My body is broken,
Not my spirit.

My mind tries to hide those things
that it thinks my heart can't handle.

Darkness

6/15/2018

You go outside
on a sunny day, thinking
you're there all alone.

Nobody can see you now,
but you sense something is different or wrong.

Your silhouette
is pictured on the ground behind you.
It is showing evidence
that you're not just there standing,
being prone.

Is the shadow your truer self,
or is there something more intriguing going on?

You see, the sun has just burned you.
You have nowhere left to turn.
So the truth of the matter that you've found here is
that in the presence of light,
your darkness
will always be shown.

The shadow is like a vision of the soul. It can only be seen when it is brought to light. Is the shadow showing us that we need to make changes in our lives so we will cast light? Are you ready to stand before the light? Remember, there is no darkness in heaven.

Untitled Desperations

8/27/2018

Battling mind,
Holding on,
Looking back,
Scared beyond perception.

Rain pouring,
Falling sand
Sifting away,
Chilling my pursuit of perfection.

Retching,
Broken,
Disemboweled,
Distressing operation.

Hopeless,
All-consuming,
Broken paths,
Complete misdirection.

Smiling,
Laughing,
Gesturing,
Masquerading behavioral disposition.

Pain,
Fear,
Disbeliefs
Stopping good intention.

Scraps,
Despair
Unappeasable,
Causing unquenchable starvation.

Lost,
Misleading,
No escape,
Creating dislocation.

Running,
Screaming,
Breathing inconsistently,
A form of strangulation.

Shipwrecked,
Castaway,
Flooded,
Misinterpretation.

Scary,
Frightful,
Ghastly things,
Mental petrifaction.

Gagging,
Choking,
Stranglehold.
Now comes suffocation.

Rasping,
Tattered,
Stretching out,
Calling out for salvation.

Fire,
Fueling,
Burning now,
A form of conciliation.

Crying,
Reaching forth,
Unimaginable things.

Untitled desperations!

This is a reminder to myself that I need the continual love and patience from my savior. I still have to fight some battles even though I'm saved. It keeps me humble.

The Flame

10/1/2018

I am the flame burning inside you.
I am fueled by your breath, the air.
I dance with the wind that surrounds you
while whispering,
"With Me, you'll find no fear."
I'll consume the darkness around you,
flickering,
"I am always here."
Smoke can only trail Me.
I bring enlightenment when you are in fear.
I will not burn you into submission.
In time, illusions become clear.
There is no disguise that can make Me hide.
Light is my second name.
There is no pretense to find Me,
for I am truly known as the flame!

This love

6/21/19

With my love to you, Katie and Derek,
this love sprang from the kind of friendship
that we all should have the joy to experience.
This love has survived time and extreme distance,
proving in its genesis
that true love will always prevail.
This love is one
we should all model our relationships after.
It's balanced, both sides giving unselfishly.
This love is openly nourished.

It will not only shine, it will flourish.
This love has brought together
two of the best souls that this world has to offer.
This love is trust, thoughtfulness, and understanding.
It is full with the ripeness of dedication.
This love already has years invested in it
with common goals that are set to be accomplished.
This love is all of us here gathered together
with open arms, so proud
just to be a part of it.
This love is one in which we all can share,
but the best part of this love is
that on this day,
a new chapter to it is just beginning.

A Turning Tide

1/19/2000

Pain raises our oceans' depth
until it finds and opens our eyes,
the doors to our souls.
Once opened, it comes in waves,
and it's unrelenting
as the tides begin to flow.
And they will not dry until the pain subsides.
It's in its healing
that all tides will withdraw.
When the tides have turned,
the lesson we've learned
is that pain was never meant to be held
inside anyone's heart or soul.

Ecstasy

5/13/1996

Ecstasy
is feeling everything openly and fully.
Sometimes it's all at once.
Ecstasy
is continually sending out a silent confirmation
of a love that is everlasting.
It's also warming, soothing, and relaxing
someone's heightened and intensified needs.
Then it's reminding them you'll do it all again,
and again and again!

Endeavor to Persevere

7/16/2018

I strive daily to live my life
the very best I can.
And I fail miserably
every day
because I am just a common man.

When I try to run away
from my sins,
it feels like I'm running in a pit of sand.

What chance do I have
to save my life
unless I fight
to hold that light
that's growing here
inside me?

I know my cries for help
reach Your merciful ears,
because I can see You
in everything
and feel You
drawing me ever so near.

All that I can do now
as flesh and bone
is to let my soul
endeavor
to persevere.

No one receives knowledge
until they want it
and are ready to handle it,
no matter what direction or form it comes in.

Evaluate yourself every day,
and you'll stay level.

A broken heart is not hurt because of delusions.
It's only found truth from the very thing that breaks it.

Lies or truth,
Stress or peace,
Love or hate—
It's always your decision.

Bless family, friends, strangers.
Make sure you're also blessed,
or you'll never be able to bless others.

Man didn't learn how to fly by watching birds.
He learned how to fly only when he stopped holding down his own
imagination.

Mindset to Move Us

1/26/2019

When lightning strikes,
it speaks the truth.
Whirlwinds scatter things,
then they can bring on clarity.
Although confused,
we can see through the disguise
of a disaster cloaked in the darkest cloth.
Dandelions seeds scatter
in the breeze,
off into new existence.
Creation never starves
if pursuing salvation.
Famine covers the land.
Left perplexed,
water always comes
from the distance.
All winds are invisible,
but their mindset is to move us.

Another Goodbye

You have the kind of friendship
that has no end,
until you have to part ways
with a childhood friend.
Off into your own adventures in life.
Too young to understand your oncoming strife.
You hug, kiss, and start to cry.
One of many yet to come,
a parade of goodbyes.

No longer a baby,
their first day of school.
One of the hardest moments
that can seem too cruel.
They've developed past infancy;
you enjoyed those years,
until you wave them along
and fight back your tears.
One moment of joy
that you can't deny.
A heartbreak that changes you,
a bittersweet goodbye.

A sudden change in the health
of one whom you love.
A call needing answered
from far up above.
There's none stopping
an oncoming noon.
A life will be cut short;
one is leaving too soon.
One of the hardest to take;
you are left wondering why.
This is one of the toughest,
heartbreaking goodbyes.

Every knee will be bent.
Every head shall be bowed.
All will be risen,
all voices aloud.
A joyous occasion
on earth and in heaven.
The congregation of all,
another goodbye continued.

Sisters and brethren, no voices will crack, no eyes will be dry. All hearts
will be singing, "There will never be another goodbye."

Unbalanced, Removed, and Reaching

1/31/2019

A pendulum on the swing does not keep precise time if it's out of balance. If being countered causes it to stop and it does not tick, there is still time.

A shadow removed will reappear again and again, devoid of any malice. It will still reach out daily though unable, trying to touch the warmth and the light from the sun.

A beggar lacking one hand still reaches out, wanting the coin that might be presented. If he hides his cache from those who give, would that be considered underhanded?

Pedestal

Every day, I fail to live up to the act that has saved me.
Every day, I sin in a number of ways.
My thoughts and my body betray me,
even though the laws have shown me the way.
I am not perfect, and I never will be.
I have the fights and the struggles
that all Christians must face.
Balance is the key to living,
and believing is key to my faith.
I cuss, I have impure thoughts,
I covet things that aren't mine,
and my soul constantly fights with my mind.
Don't place me on a pedestal because I will fail you,
and those expectations are unfair to me.
I can only walk with my weaknesses
and pray for all of my mistakes.
I'm no one to look up to.
I'm only an example of one who has found salvation
through His blood and by God's abundance of grace.

A Mountain

9/5/2018

I am a mountain!
I am majestic, strong, and silent.
I am also humble enough
that I will allow myself to be eroded
and broken down
into a lot of pieces before you.

The modest stones within and around myself
are coming back together in silence, to bring everyone peace.
We are collectively rejoining our ranks, to allow you
and others to walk over us.

Sacrificing is our task, so we united,
forming this sand.

We created this beach to serve every soul
who is searching to find peace of mind
and comfort by the ocean.

Now it's time to discover how rare
and precious we are,
even though our numbers seem to be countless.

Although they might not see it or understand it,
We are giving rise and opening minds to a slower pace
while encouraging everyone to see the symbolism.

Now we are stronger, settled into our new place in life,
where some will perceive us only as being soft and little.
Underfoot, others won't notice us at all.

You see, most people's vision will lack our depth
inasmuch as they hold onto stereotypes
and other misconceptions.

Those who are suffering from illusions and erosions to their sight
are crippled with a blurred spiritual perception.

At this moment in time, the illusion is
I appear to be scattered, unassuming, and minimal.

If you only look at my appearance
from a narrow impious point of view,
indeed it is verily true.
My image currently changed.

But if you look at my essence once again, you'll see
that I remained the same.

You see, size can be sacrificed symbolically,
and that size doesn't make one proverbial.

Now I am eminent, because I live and speak of this truth
while knowing you will see only what you want to see.

But if you choose to see the open humility
engrained in my heart, you will see that when I'm humble.
I may appear to be at my least,
but those subtle moments in my life
prove I never stopped being a mountain.

November Ghosts

1/26/2019

Alone in the forest before the dawn, the trees hold fleeing secrets. The voices of the residents collide as the sun slowly rises. The crackling of the leaves start calling to the hunters that are there in waiting. Some are deceived by falling acorns and the squirrels off in the distance.

The November ghosts appear only when hunters are not looking. The strings from their bows trick their eyes when focusing on the vitals. Their scent gives away all of their attempts to hide in their well-thought-out locations.

It is important for them to realize they disappear as quickly as they surface. The tidal wave crashes in when it comes to light; the season has already ended.

The November ghosts have won again this epic yet subtle confrontation, leaving all hearts involved thumping and furiously beating.

Oceans

1/29/2019

I stand looking at the waves in the ocean. Then I look up at the sky. I see that both are blue, and the peaks on the waves are like those in the clouds in the sky above me.

I think I want to swim and fly in both.
When I do, won't they give me a feeling of peace, a newfound feeling of freedom?

I can find peace in the waves or the winds, or I can find fear if either comes rushing in.

I have to hold or lose my breath to swim in either. Why, oh why is the feeling the same? I can't fathom the depth in either ocean, or the depth of this subject.

It looks like I'll sink in one and fly in the other, but if I stand my ground in between both of them, I realize I'm soaring when I'm in either one. They are parted by a spiritual mirror. One is a reflection of the other. Will my hands seem to wave as I swim, and fly in either of these oceans?

I find these two oceans as mirrors of each other, and it's mind-provoking that they have similar characteristics. Both the sky and the ocean have vast depth. You have to fly to be in the sky, and you feel like you're flying when you swim in the ocean. To be able to dwell in the sky (heaven), you need to die and lose your breath. To swim in the depth of the ocean, like you would in the sky, you must also lose (hold) your breath. It's just another set of God's wonders that leave me breathless.

Diamonds, They Last Forever

10/10/1996

I was a piece of coal,
trying to hide behind my sins
and the color that filled me.

I was there until the One came along,
searching, and found me.

When He did, He asked
if I'd let Him into
the deepest part of my chest,
just so He could make me
into a better man.

I said "yes."
Since then,
I've been changing every day
and in every way
as He chisels away
at my worldly nature.

That constant transformation
helps to keep my heart pure,
just like a white diamond.
Every day, He polishes me
to heal all wounds this cruel world has
and will give me.

It causes me to shine
as His precious stone,
so I'll reflect all of the colors of His rainbow.

That makes me a symbol
of the hues He's used
to represent both the love
and covenant between us.

Now, it's impossible for this world to hide
or break me.

I could have stayed the same way
that I was when He found me,
but I'd just be nothing more
than a piece of fuel that will eventually be fed
into the eternal lake of fire.

That reminds me of the saying
about both heaven and hell
that's also used for diamonds,

They last forever!

Sin and the soul are represented as a piece of coal. We choose whether we are to be saved and become diamonds, or whether we are to live and die full of sin.

If we find salvation, we become transformed into beings reflecting light. It's then that we can reflect His love like a rainbow to all of those around us. Each day, He lifts us up and polishes away our problems, and that lets us shine.

God promised that He loved us so much that He would never flood the world again. After He said that, He gave us a symbol in the sky to remind us of that promise. That promise is His rainbow.

What do most of us give as a promise to love someone forever in marriage? It's a ring with a diamond on it. It's a symbol of the greatest emotional gift we can give, and it reflects the colors of the rainbow.

Love is by far strongest emotional gift that we can give to others. The diamond is the strongest physical object we can give.

Is it a coincidence that we were led to give a symbol that reflects the colors of the rainbow to represent our promise to love forever in marriage? Is it odd that both are symbols that promise an eternal love? Is it just chance? Diamonds do what? They last forever! It's just like heaven and hell: they last forever. Become a diamond and shine!

I keep my mind moving
because I never want the dust to settle.
Great event?
Finding purpose …

Until Religion restricts…
Spirituality frees …

I don't want to climb the ladder.
I don't even want to see the ladder.
However, I do want to go up.

Passion for oneself and others is living at its best.

Let your heart delight in each moment.

Your soul sees what your eyes can't.

Weakness causes a feeling of discomfort.
Strength causes a feeling of ease.

Communication is paramount
for your survival with others and yourself.

Be introspective.
Be honest about everything that concerns yourself.
If you are honest and see yourself as you really are,
and why you are the way you are, you will have fewer problems with yourself
and others.

If you want to climb a tree
and are unsure how to do it,
do you trust yourself? Maybe the tree
doesn't want you to fall.
Is this really about a tree?
Trust yourself,
so you can climb up
and have a higher perspective.
Is this really about a tree?

A Rose and an Empty Hand

1/31/2019

I see rose is still a rose,
even if she is decaying.
To the soil she must return,
to a different state of being.

She whispers with her last breath,
"You, you are more than my friend.
Before I disappear, my love,

I cry out for you to pick me up.
I can't leave you here empty-handed."

To which I reply,
"Don't worry for me, my love.
My life's not spent using the banker's coin.
My heart abounds.
It is satiated.
Because of you, I'm more than wealthy.
I don't need to hold you in my hands, to feel your worth, my love.
My heart already holds the
treasure of your beauty!"

Some things don't need to be held to appreciate its beauty. It could be a butterfly, a bird, or the love that you have for another. When you love another, you should hold your love for them in your heart. Don't restrict or put limitations on your loved ones. Allow them to grow. Don't pluck them from their places in the world where they are growing, thinking that their beauty is only for you.

We are all made for everyone we encounter. No matter how big or how small the moment is, it leaves impressions. We leave footprints. We have an obligation to share our love and that beauty of each moment. Real value is not in material things or things we can hold in our hands. Worth is in the heart.

On one side, my friend loves me and does not want to die leaving me feeling empty. I don't want her to leave my presence without her knowing that I appreciate her love, and that I love her too. She had her impact on my life. So I'm telling her that she has already touched my heart with her life, and that she is a treasure in my heart. We should never leave others' presence without expressing concern for their state of being or letting them know they are loved and cherished. We should also let others know that they are loved for who they are, not for what they can give us.

Impending Doom

9/9/2018

Mind is rank
Soul is solemn

Body's dank
Empty cavern

Obscurity bites
Lonely trial

Losing faith
In denial

There is no voice
Only hush

Absent light
Barely dusk

Needing relief
Confused and rattled

Struggling grief
Constant battle

Spiritual theft
Conceding gloom

What is left?
Impending doom …

God's Greatest Masterpiece

7/22/2018

We have all heard
and seen great creations,
from beautiful music to beautiful art.
But the greatest, the most beautiful thing
that anyone can create
can only come from inside their hearts.
The greatest thing I know of in all of creation is love.
So I contemplate what I believe to be God's
next greatest creation that sits far up above.
Staring at an amazing night's sky,
I see an endless array of planets and stars.
It's amazing to see what He has done.
I try to draw a parallel between these two things.
I try my best to comprehend it.
I witness that this night sky
is only a small representation of His love
that is so splendid.
I have seen that His love has no end.
It is deeper, and it continually fills.
I also understand that I'm unworthy and incapable
of describing such events of love,
but maybe someday, if I'm blessed enough, I will.

Hope

7/6/2001

Hope is always a wonderful gift to give someone.
It always comes in a beautiful package.
It doesn't cost a dime.
And it's always priceless.

Forbidden Fruit

1/24/2019

Watch the box. Watch the box.
The apple has raised its head.
Man has eaten from the forbidden fruit;
now knowledge is his sin.

Reset, repeat. I'll say it again.
From His seed, all of man
is eating away at God's forbidden fruit.
Why is there this new technology?

Once colored as a rainbow,
the new shade fades to gray.
To dine on that which monitors
all your moves
is to also hasten an early grave.
Do you pause before you enter?

Don't trade away every line.
You can delete only on the surface.
It is written in your script.
It will catch you when you lie,
even if you don't move your lips.
Are you pretending? Are you acting?

The fruit, the fruit is a false god,
one of which we all have bitten.
The bite of man has spilled the juice
upon each face and in every land.
A synthetic memory still fooling man.
Where do the pictures go?

There's a tracking of every stroke.
I hear answers from the devil's throat.
He is attempting to be the true All Knowing,
but he will fail to inherit that task.

The apple, the apple can only proceed
if it has false light, the source, or your spark.
Don't bite from the apple you see before you,
or you'll end up in eternity, lost in the dark!

Ask yourself why technology really uses a fruit as its logo. It could be a representation for the forbidden fruit. I do believe the original sin gave the gift of knowledge. The apple icon is used for the world leader in technology at the time of this being written. That logo is used for all phones and computers in movies. Why? Think about the connection!

Forgiveness

2/1/2019

I'm not free unless I free the chains
of wrong intentions
to create keys of forgiveness.

I am not saved unless I swim to the shore
with waves of glory splashing over me.
I must make it to the shore
to stand there in forgiveness.

Together, on the bush thorns and roses
are discrepancies of the other.
Together, on the bush
they both hold equal beauty.
If I reach out to touch it without caution,
I'm sure to feel the sting of the bee
protecting their love.
In that bite, I apologize.
I ask the plant for forgiveness.

If a bird's wing breaks,
Its elegance will still fly.
It is not arrogance when they soar.
If I dissolve this paint from the earth or sky,
will I ever find my forgiveness?

Dancing in the Light

7/7/2018

Can you still picture the rays of sunshine that came through the window panes when you were a child? Did you inspect them any closer when you saw them? Did you see anything more?

I did. I saw little specks of dust floating delicately in the air. They were there moving up and down, left and right, leaving me feeling safe and warm.
It looked as if they were dancing to an inaudible sound being emitted from the light. Was there a song playing that only they could hear? I believe they were dancing only because they were in the light, and that light is the song of heaven.

Point of the Axis

1/31/2019

We must look at this world using the eyes that we used as a child standing in innocence, to see all of God's glory.

We must look at diamonds shining tirelessly as God's love melts them in the sun. As children, we use that sight to watch the spikes point toward their destiny. They disappear somewhere in the snow. Icicles glow for a reason.

When looking at a rainbow, we remind ourselves that this world can only bend God's light.

We must look at flowers once again, using a child's sight, while pulling their petals off to be sure that God's buds, once removed, still hold their beauty.

We must look with children's eyes to look through our own dust on the mirror. We must do it to make sure that our resemblance still mimics our every movement.

We must use childlike eyes to see that His eyes are the principal point of the axis.

Dreaming big is the only way to dream.
If you don't, you are not dreaming.

We are part of the universe.
We just need to reconnect to it.

On behalf of my mind,
I apologize if I didn't see you or your needs clearly.

Everything is evidence,
So seek …

Truth is!

Why?
Always ask why.
Why?
Because you learned the most in your life that you could when you were a
child, because you asked why.
Isn't that the ultimate question?

No one can truly see from your perspective,
even if you agree on what you see.

Never be embarrassed by your past
Unless you continue to live it.

If you ever stop growing up,
You are no longer living.

To say you no longer love another who is far away
Is admittance that you never really loved them.
You don't have to keep them directly in your life
To love them.

Fool's Gold

6/25/2018

For countless years,
men have sacrificed their lives
to find the one thing in life
that mimics both the warmth
and the beauty of light that comes from the sun.

They need to look deep into their chests
to realize the totality of their circumstance.

They are left not knowing
something is wrong.

Gold is just a rock!

In the end, he will see
it'll be the great cause of his destruction.

Its totals won't amount to much
when you consider the price of salvation.

They don't see that there is no cost to accept
that Christ has died so that we can all be free.

The devil has made his mark
on all of our hearts as we struggle
and live in vain, just because
we think we will be more comfortable.

Earth spins around and around again.
Another chance for us all
to gain all of the real riches
that can never be taken away.

If you have invested too much into this place,
your soul will have no chance for advancement.

Only the beguiled have invested their lives
so deep into this world that it is enough,
that they will spend endless time dwelling
in the shallows for fool's gold!

Gold mimics the light of the sun. The sun is a symbol of the Son. Gold is the backbone of earthly treasuries. Jesus is the backbone of heavenly treasure. Some can say it's just a coincidence that gold shines like the sun, and because of it, we value it more than anything else. Maybe man was led to find and treasure something that shines like the sun for a reason. Is this a worldly lesson linking us back to God? If that rock is all we seek as we walk through life, is it really worth it? We can't take it with us when we die.

Life: just lessons that lead us back to Him.

Am I just a thought? An idea?
Is every thought its own universe?

I pray that when you see me, you see Him.

The Promise

12/31/2019

I shall cherish this rain, this storm,
because if I endure, one day I will blossom
from the promise that comes with it.

Unless you first have a light burning within you,
you cannot shine outwardly.

These Five Things

3/24/2019

In your ear,
I want to be the whisper,
The one whom you listen to.

In your mind,
I want to be the answer,
The one whom you do not have to question.

In your heart,
I want to be your love,
The one whom you trust enough to accept.

In your eyes,
I want to be the vision,
The one whom you don't forget.

In your soul,
I want to be the fire,
The one who burns without end.

I want to be included in these five things,
Involved in everything that you do.
I want you to believe in Me,
I give you My promise
That I will always deliver.
I Am the Truth …

Questioning

7/6/2018

Who
exactly are you to me?
You are more than just my King.
What
have I ever done for you,
to cause you to be so kind to me?
When
will you come for me?
How much time do I have left?
Why
do you show me all these things that I never knew,
so I don't have to continue to guess?
Where
does your mercy end?
I'll need it before my last breath.

You're always so good to me,
even when I break all of Your laws.

I'll never stop questioning you,
and I know that
You'll never stop giving me answers.

You are all that I need.
You are my only Master.
Will I believe in and continue to follow You?
That is Your only question.

Growth is induced by
Destruction of complacency.

At times, distance is a necessity
To keep love from fading.

The dawning of a new day is an awakening of the mind.
The wakening is awarded with new tests.
Tests are for strengthening faith.
Faith is to be tested every day to keep you strong enough to spiritually
survive any mistakes you make.

Isolation is my safe place for deep thinking.
Deep thoughts extinguish my fears.
Conquering fears gives me peace.
It allows me to let others back in.

Kiss each morning,
Greeting the new steps that you have to take each day.

We're all lights.
Appreciate each other's ability to shine.

Never tell someone what to do,
Ask them instead,
And you'll see the difference a few simple words make.

Giving brings you more than you've given away.

Hate is a disease of the heart
That can only be healed by love.

Your circle of life does not confine you in it.
Learn to live on the never-ending edge
To find the never-ending joy that resides only on the fringes.

Poetry in Motion

6/2/1995

At the heart of the lake,
there was a need.
So the answer formed a drop of grace.
Then it fell as rain from heaven.

After feeling that poetry
that was set into motion,
the rhythm lost most of its mystery.

We can overcome all of the obstacles
coming into and out of our lives,
if we can just recognize them
as they come in their many forms.

The Master Poet
is always writing His creative answers.
They are continually pouring down.

By not allowing ourselves to see them
as they're streaming forth,
we are just asking for a life that is full of storms!

And if we let a shower move our way,
it is promised that our waters will be moved.

It flows through me so much
that I can't hold it inside.
I'm constantly being moved by its Maker.

I'm a ripple in His wake,
yet I'm calmer than ever before.

But my peace is not placid.
Therefore, my pulse of harmony is always moving,
and within that melody, we should take note
that none of us is ever alone.

I hear rhyming so full of love above me
that I'm no longer satisfied by the depth of this pool.
So I'm keeping my eyes skyward
as I seek my new home in that profound ocean above me.
And I'm willing to spill over as many banks as it takes
until I finally get there.

Many can feel me moving now,
That I'm poetry in His book of life.
For it is He
who has set me
in motion!

Hourglass

6/25/2018

Look at the sand inside the hourglass. It demands your undivided attention. But don't look past the intricacies of this invention. If you are in a desert, a sandstorm can come along your path, causing you to lose your way. Or you could die, lost in all of that dust.

You can also melt sand, making it into something new that will allow the nearly blind to see. You can make a pair of glasses, or if you want, you might view the hourglass as only a timing invention, used to keep track of your life as it simply passes away.

God takes you through the trials in your life so that He can heat you up, just like an hourglass. It makes your actions, and your heart appear clear to Him. He can see inside your heart just like He's looking at that glass. He can always look deep enough to detect your deepest intentions.

Sand can either blind you or give you the ability to see. I would call it irony if you can't see the truth in this lesson that man was led to create this invention as a tool to teach us about life and the power of our awesome God. We naturally live these lessons as proof that there is no excuse for not knowing there is a God.

Not having to be worthy of love
Is the very thing that makes love so incredible.
We are all part of humankind.
If you've given up on humankind.
You've given up on yourself as well.

When you see yourself improving,
You are further along than you realize.

When success has surpassed your humility,
You have badly misstepped.

Dreams are only the beginning.
Allow them to lead you on to much more.

Yes, I should, but will I?

Find the path. Walk the path
To find its end,
Your beginning ...

Release
Exhaust frustrations.
Move within each moment.
Accept time;
With it, peace is yours to find.

You are what you are aware of.

The heart understands everything it needs to know.
Release your inner peace. Whisper from your soul.

Freedom must be taken in all instances

Before shooting for the stars.
Remind yourself you are already among them.

01

7/12/2018

Our digital world has brought us space-age technology, leading us to almost anything we wish to know. We have open access to limitless information coming in from all over the globe.

The Internet is an entity, like a ghost. You can't really see it, and you can't go far as to call it the All Knowing, but if you want, you could probably come somewhere very close.

Can you see the imitator of God? Do you know what all of the codes are about? Does the gargantuan momentum of this technology leave you in doubt?

Binary codes are used to program all computers. They are made up by only using the numbers zero and one. Where does all the information go when we are done?

He is trying to replace God. Maybe we should always keep this in mind: one is always greater than zero. The devil is always the zero. God always has been and always will be the one!

Destiny to Cleanse

2/6/2019

I open the faucet to let the droplets beat on my skin. This rhythm, it soothes me.

I listen for each drum pulsing, beating, and pounding on my flesh, forming waterways some will simply transcend.

Some crossing, some parallel, some never meeting on roads as they travel upon my body. Some come together to face the drain, once released from my skin.

I try to feel each individual working its way from my head to my toes. I listen to nothing but those drops, and eventually I start relaxing. Yes, I give in.

When I realize they are a symbol to my mind, my soul, I weep. I'm free to feel their purpose. They are there to service me without and within. And their destiny, their purpose is only to cleanse.

Patience and Faith

The long chase
is off in the distance.
The light, the nourishment,
punishes the strength of waste.

The blackness does not scare me,
although those blankets have certainly tried.

I scoured for proof of Your existence
in the mountains, the forest, and the plains.

I found Your star rising.
My fears are ready to be slain.

The splendors of Your teachings are tender.
I revel in Your grace.
To Your love I surrender.
You have forged my heart to exist
with patience and in faith.

Blinding Light

7/19/2018

The snow had covered the land.
The miracle of winter was at hand.
The unearthly light from the snow
was blinding me from everything I'd known.
I started to realize that the light
was killing the life of a year's worth of worldly sin.

The crystals pointing down were the snow's way
of showing me that spring was about to begin.
I saw that anything covered in light long enough
has a second chance to live.

Being in the light is the only way
to become blind to this world of sin.
Salvation blinds your sight to the world
as it opens you up to a life
that only its pure and blinding light can give.

Remember how hard it was to see when you came in from being outside after playing in the snow? Snow is like purity. It's innocent and unblemished. Was it the innocence of childhood that allowed you to notice the rainbow of lights, created by the sun as it bounced off of the icicles in the first place? If you don't notice them as an adult, maybe you should ask yourself why. Once you see light, do you really need to see anything more?

The Same Name

6/22/1999

Man used to think that the sun, the moon, and all of the stars revolved around him and his world. Eventually, we've learned that this was the furthest thing from the truth. Now we know that the warmth and light from the sun is what gave each of us a mortal life. We know that our world really revolves around the sun.

Over time, people have had to individually learn that the only way to gain an eternal life is by not allowing their lives to revolve around themselves or their world. They had to let their lives revolve around the Son, but it's the One who is also called Christ!

Each man should bow his head and forever walk in shame if he thinks that it's only a coincidence that the givers of each type of life are pronounced by words with the same sounding name: the sun and the Son!

***

Realizing a life revolving around the sun/Son is how life is meant to be a powerful lesson. I've had to struggle to learn this. I still do. God's grace is the only reason I will make it to heaven and why my life revolves around His Son. Both sun and Son are givers of life. Both are to be revolved around to accomplish this feat. One is a natural life lesson. The other is a natural spiritual life lesson.

I know that the names sun/Son only sound the same in English. I will respond by saying that English has become the most spoken language by fate for a reason. Another non-coincidence. There is a reason why this lesson works.

My mind is consumed by chaos.
It has yet to be conquered.

Imagination:
The beginning of potential.

Honest, open communication
Is the key to all problems within oneself
And concerning any interactions with others.

Déjà vu:, the recognition of the moment.

I don't expect everyone to understand my depth.
Some are not yet ready.
I'm not ready to go as deep as I can go either.

Love does not need an explanation.
Love on either side is acceptance.
When you or unbelievers find love,
It all comes from God.
It is the very proof of His existence.
Love is a force that is beyond explanation.
If you are a pebble on the beach,
You are also part of the whole.
Does it matter how small you are?
The only thing of importance is
That you are really whole.

The moon is in the dark.
The sun is in the light.
Both are always singing.

The Winds That I Must Follow

1/2/1997

At times,
I stand against the winds
that others choose to follow.
Then again,
I let others take me
to those other places
where so very few have ever gone.
But I'm not free to take my journeys
until I face my life's inner struggle.
Daily my body tries to deny me
the Breath of Life,
which is the very thing
my soul endeavors to swallow.
I find it is always a subtle breeze
that blossoms any seeds of my wisdom.
And that is where I humbly search
for those great mysteries
I am so graciously allowed to harvest.
My God,
I have found nothing but love,
truth,

and peace
when You have given me
the winds
that I must follow.

One day, I was trying to feel God's will while standing against the stronger blowing winds and while letting the lighter, gentler winds lead me in their directions. In that moment, I felt His will, and He told me this is how He would show me His mysteries, if I would simply follow His gentle persuasions (the winds). He told me to stand against the ways of the world (the stronger winds), and I would find Him.

He told me I would see proof of His existence through symbolic lessons, but I'm flawed. I don't always let the gentle winds move me. I'm weak. I follow the ways of the world too. So He told me it's always my choice in how I choose to learn.

My greatest joys come from His gentle urging and following those urges. Some are so gentle that I'm unaware of their presence; I don't notice their impact on my future until years later. I am gently asking anyone who reads this to go with the flow and let the gentle winds lead you. May you find love, truth, and peace as I have.

Inspiration

9/14/202

There is a great persistence in a calling.
A duty comes with the onset of inspiration in one's spirit.
If you feel it, catch it at once. It is fleeting.
The responsible ones realize it is not a gift to be caged;
It is to be cherished, admired, and recognized
For all its worth, and then it is to be released.
That's when souls are replenished,
And it has value only when it is shared.

In those moments, feel the pain. Feel the joy. Life.
It is!

Encounter,
Embrace,
Love.

The mind powers the pen. The pen empowers the reader's mind.
Finding peace within yourself brings you peace with others.

Living is dancing in the absence of music.

I will hold my breath no more. I will breathe in the scent of my maker. I
choose to live.

Being confounded by the world is the only state of mind where you can
find God, approach Him, and love Him with reverence.

I must dance in humility to know I have seen light.

Inside, inside of the inside is the only place I need to be.

May I listen to the temple that is my soul.

Love is set to blind your mind and make your heart see.

Keep watching. The sun is always shining even if you are not in a place
to see it.

The Leaving of Leaves

1/4/1996

Descending
from their climax.
Cascading
to the ground.
Peaking
in a crescendo.
Falling
without a sound.
Displaying
brilliant colors after spending
a season basking in the sun.
The effects
are all magnificent.
They are all offered to everyone.
They served above us before,
and below us now.
It's only when sacrificing their lives
that their voices will sound.
Crackling as we walk over them,
they say the only words they are to speak.
"Sometimes, we must make sacrifices
for the ones that we love.
We're all coming back to see you again next spring.
But we're only coming back here to remind you of this,
so please hear us each time as we leave!"

All we have to do to see God's promises is pay attention to nature with an open heart and open mind.

A seed sprouts and begins to grow. The tree spends its energy and strength to continue to reach for the light.

The highest limbs resist the earth's gravitational pull and grow the closest to being straight up.

The lowest limbs don't fight for light as well. They grow outward taking the easiest way out. They are too slow to reach for the light.

The leaves play a part too. They are made to soak up the light. They do this until the season changes. As they start to die, they change their color.

The color change is a way for the tree to show you that if you spend enough time in your spiritual light, you will become more beautiful. Then you can begin playing your part by spreading your light to all with whom you come in contact.

Soon, the leaves start making noises as the wind blows, while nature prepares us for the cold that is to come. The leaves try to get your attention as they struggle for light.

Eventually, they start making noises in the wind, yelling at us to watch. Finally they give up their last bit of life by falling and calling out to us.

They scream out as we walk over them for us to look at all the beauty that came from devoting our lives to the light. Now we can help provide new life all around us, and for the tree we came from. So please hear us each time as we leave.

Stop, and think how our lives are like the leaves and family branches. We are of little use if we don't reach for the light of the sun/Son. If you allow the light in, you will be beautiful and people will watch you as you spread your life's light.

A family tree is just like any tree in nature. If either type of tree reaches for the light they will grow. If a storm comes by (trials in life), the wind will knock off any weak branches (people being tried). It's usually the lower fatter branches (those not following God's law) that get killed off first by breaking away from the tree. The lower branches didn't fight enough against gravity and wind, (sin). So they die first. They are the furthest ones from the light (salvation). They are the sinners. Don't most criminals die first? They are the weak branches. Don't become a weak limb!

Tsunami

1/23/2019

I Am the tsunami,
professing the surge of power before you.
My will is as the light.
I Am songs sung, as violent whispers
even to those
not acknowledging My existence.
I Am the source, the force beyond sight.
Come sing with Me.
The swells are your guide.
I exist patiently,
waiting for your love.
I give mine freely.
Surrender to each wave.
You will not die.
Each wave is a welcoming wave of life.
I Am more than the ocean.

Those who love you are watching, waiting for you to circle their world. Bring your light with you. Shine …

We are all beautiful, individual snowflakes hitting the window. All will melt.

Daily you are thirsty.
Daily you are hungry.
Quench your soul daily.

The balance of nature is incredible.
Do not be a part that throws it out of sync.

Become the patron of essence. Feel your purpose.
Let your destiny flow.

Primal, experience, childhood.
Vision, innocence, no fear.
Conscious of everything.
Calm, excited, no fear.
Aging, beware of fear.

I've been disabled so I can see the mercy
In my trials to strengthen my beliefs.
You are the source of existence.
In my portion, I have gained my purpose,
A nibble of your strength.

The moon stays.
The sun stays.
You are to stay in the source of light …

Self love should be your first love.

Consciousness is acceptance, expansion of the mind, an awakening with no forgiveness, a vision for the formally blind.

Dreams

9/14/2018

Blankets, covered eyes.
I sleep.

Looking, striving, reaching out.
Which dreams do I keep?

Awake, solemn,
lifted soul.

Grasping, pulling at dreams.
Are they mine to control?

Memories, purposely faint,
or bad.

Crying, sobbing, total fear.
It's those that tend to scare me.

Shallow, discontent,
unraveling.

Are some really that weak?

Confused, at a loss,
disconnected.

I can't find my way home.
This is a terrible dream. I'm lost.

Horror, falling, from the sky.
Where do I go from here?
Is this the dream where I die?

The monster, lusting,
hungry for me.

This monster is chasing me again!
I fear that I can't lock the door!

Sighing, yawning,
finding relief.
Eyes red and opened wide,

The Voice told me
nothing can hurt me here.
He said that they were only dreams!

Then He said these six comforting words to me:
"All is not what it seems."

Always

1/18/2019

Time is always unsurprised when facing the faces on the clocks.

Thorns are always fierce when protecting the rose.
They do not pretend by blossoming.

No matter in which direction the music beats, the rock doesn't miss its note. No, it is set in stone.

A seed will even settle where there is no dust, in a place that seems to lack any hope. Yes, a seed in the breeze will find itself a home. Are you strong enough to grow?

Always
face,
protect,
direct.
When you settle things with your loved ones, then your love will grow stronger.

Listen to your soul. It never lies.

A day without thoughts of you
is a day without love.
I have a great life because you are part of it

Think about this.
The sun will blind you if you try to look directly at it,
but it will always show you the way.

We have yet to capture the glory of the sun
through eyes or invention.

Even dead-end roads lead to somewhere.

God is not bound by a religion.

The Root of All Evil

6/26/2018

Every child is born as close as they'll ever be to a life without sin. They are also born with a mouth full of fresh breath; it's an almost a perfectly clean scent. Even when they release their food, it is little redolence.

Our teenage years bring us closer to this world.
And as we start pulling away from God's light, the time comes when our bodies start letting out odors and oils, because we are starting to lose the promise that comes with innocence.

We start to crave those things that carnal knowledge brings. We move on with life, and then we begin to increase our amount of sin. We start to produce more odors that come along with sin.

Our bodies are filled with contamination and sinfulness.
This is not just a show; it's evidence of another test while we fight for our souls. All of us become corrupted. We fail our heavenly Father by not doing what is in our best interest.

We chase this world as adults, trying to gain all of its riches, and we try to find the proof of the fact that heaven does or does not truly exists.

Now it's time to unveil another of the devil's tricks.
It's just a weakened act of collusion. He never shows his one true face. He only uses his skills, lies, and illusions. Why is it that this world also runs on oil?

How come the richest men control our lives by gaining money on everything that we work for? Why is it that the color of oil is also the color of sin? What causes us all to fall away from our true Lord's mighty grip?

Most money comes from oil, and it's malevolence. The lessons about each type of oil are evidence that each leads to all things that are corrupt. I know that it's not another coincidence, and I know that it's also the root of all evil!

This Rock

1/25/2019

This rock, this rock,
you've deceived us far too long.
Your wardrobe is so shiny.
The attraction is so strong.
You've fooled us with your false worth,
with the currency in which you flow.
We all have been conceding,
putting you in control.
But when we wake up,
we will find true treasure
within the true gems, within the merits found forever
in each other's souls!
Because a rock is still just a rock,
even if it appears to glow.

Enlightenment

1/27/2019

Thrust light has pierced my soul,
for I was out of balance.

The closer I get insanity,
the closer I get
to enlightenment.

Is it a crime
that I must lose my mind
to find all of the answers to my questions?

I follow the Guide that draws the lines,
to serve the Ruler
of my humble purpose.

I sift all of the grains of sand
through my hands,
looking to find my fellow man.
I don't think I'm a nomad,
alone in the desert.

The question for me
is, When will I see
my holy Maker?

The question for all I encounter is,
Can you help me answer my call,
and can we find oasis?

Inside, inside of the inside is the only place I need to be.
God is not white. He is light.

May I listen to the temple that is my soul.

Love is set to blind your mind and let your heart see.

Keep watching. The sun is always shining, even if you are not in a place
to see it.

Become the patron of essence. Feel your purpose.
Let your destiny flow.

The moon stays.
The sun stays.
So I am to stay in the source of light.

There is no existence without source.
Source has yet to be explained.

The floodgates are open.
The water does it part.
Knowledge is always descending;
It only fills open hearts.
Treasure your existence, your love.

Self-love should be your first love.

I do not try to put off tomorrow.
There is no such thing as time delay.
Time is not my master.
I am not his slave.

Consciousness is acceptance, expansion of the mind, an awakening with
forgiveness, vision for those who were blind.

Listen to your soul; it never lies.

Even before we know what we are, we are.

Be cool when others get hot,
And be warm when others are cold.
Then they'll have no one to blame.

Relief only comes when you perceive that you were in a disaster.

If man has evolved from monkeys, why and when did he come to need the existence of a creator in his heart and soul? What benefit is it to the species?

You do know the picture is still clear on the other side of the broken glass, don't you?

Waterfall of Light

2/24/1999

I see the glowing currents of light
as rivers of life

because it's as if they are pouring through His fingers
as His gentle hands begin parting the clouds.

He convinces me
with this awesome display of His strength
that His powers can't be withheld.

At other times,
He takes the clouds completely away
so I can witness all His glory.

They all come pouring down
in golden streams,
perfect in their silence.

Then they begin flooding me
as if I were the sea,
because my heart is their final destination.

Now I stand here,
undeserving,
under this waterfall of light
as I'm being washed in the warmth,
of God's love.

Mine to Hold

4/7/1998

When You created me,
You cut my life to the length of a string.
Then You used Your love and grace to warm me,
Your candle wax,
so You could mold me.

Until then, I was nothing more
than a useless piece of art
residing in the dark,
struggling
to hold on to my cord of life—
until I cried out Your holy name.

That's when You picked me up
to give me purpose by lighting the flame
that became the fire
of my identity.

Now
I understand,
as I burn away each day of my life,
that I'm not becoming anything less.
In reality, You showed me
that I'm becoming so much more.

I can see evidence of that fact
as my life begins to flow.

When I let my troubles melt away,
it frees my heart to hold more
so I can share more of Your love.

My eyes were opened
when I received Your light.
It was then that You told me
I'd be spending the rest of my life learning
to let it go.

Then You told me that my purpose in life
is to show others Your light,
because the truth is
that my life
was never mine
to hold.

Printed in the United States
By Bookmasters